ARNOLD SCHWARZENEGGER
A Little Golden Book® Biography

For Kate and Jane —D.M.

By Diana Murray
Illustrated by Alexandra Bye

 A GOLDEN BOOK • NEW YORK

Text copyright © 2024 by Diana Murray
Cover art and interior illustrations copyright © 2024 by Alexandra Bye
All rights reserved. Published in the United States by Golden Books, an imprint of
Random House Children's Books, a division of Penguin Random House LLC, 1745 Broadway,
New York, NY 10019. Golden Books, A Golden Book, A Little Golden Book, the G colophon,
and the distinctive gold spine are registered trademarks of Penguin Random House LLC.
rhcbooks.com
Educators and librarians, for a variety of teaching tools, visit us at RHTeachersLibrarians.com
Library of Congress Control Number: 2022950265
ISBN 978-0-593-64728-8 (trade) — ISBN 978-0-593-64729-5 (ebook)
Printed in the United States of America
10 9 8 7 6 5 4 3 2 1

Arnold Alois Schwarzenegger was born on July 30, 1947, in the small village of Thal in Austria. World War II had recently ended. Times were tough throughout the country, and there was little food.

Arnold shared a bedroom with his older brother, Meinhard. From their window, Arnold could see grazing cows and farmland. He wondered what else was out there. He always felt he was destined for bigger things.

Arnold's family lived on the top floor of a
very old house. There was no running water or
refrigerator. As a young boy, Arnold woke up early
to do his chores and exercise. He brought buckets
of water from the well to the house . . .

. . . got milk
from a local farm,

carried in heavy
loads of firewood,

and did sit-ups—
all before breakfast.

When Arnold had some free time, he loved going into town to watch American movies. He gazed in wonder at the tough cowboys and brave heroes on the screen. The theater also played short films called newsreels that showed news from America. He couldn't believe how tall the buildings were! America looked like such an exciting place.

From the age of ten, Arnold started telling everyone that he would move to America one day and be a movie star! Other kids laughed at him. Even the grown-ups shook their heads. They simply couldn't imagine it—but Arnold could! He knew he'd make it happen someday. He just didn't know how . . . yet.

At school, Arnold enjoyed drawing and math. He was also a bit of a joker. When he read assignments in front of the class, he loved to get a laugh out of the other students.

After school, Arnold often went to a lake near his home. A lifeguard there showed him some exercises. Arnold tried to do chin-ups on a thick tree branch, but he could only manage one or two. The lifeguard said if he practiced, he'd be able to do at least ten by the end of the summer. Arnold was amazed at how simple that sounded. All he had to do was keep trying and do a little more each time. He began training at the lake every day!

Arnold decorated his room with photos of bodybuilders and read about them in magazines. Some, like Reg Park, had also starred in American movies. Could bodybuilding be Arnold's path to becoming a movie star?

Yes! He could see it clearly in his mind.

At the age of fifteen, Arnold joined a weight
lifting club. Over time, he was able to lift heavier
and heavier weights. His muscles got bigger and
bigger. He loved being around people who shared
his passion for bodybuilding. Everything about the
sport made him happy.

When Arnold was eighteen, he served in the
Austrian army for a year. He loved big vehicles,
so he was excited to learn how to drive a tank. He
continued working out, lifting weights, and exercising
for four hours a day, in addition to his army training.

The soldiers were given hearty meals, including steak. Arnold's family rarely had meat because it was too expensive. Now he could eat as much as he wanted. The extra protein made his muscles grow even faster. He had to keep getting new uniforms in larger sizes!

After the army, Arnold got a job running a gym in Munich, Germany. He enjoyed his first taste of city life. Best of all, he was now winning major bodybuilding competitions, just like his idols! He was the youngest competitor to ever win the title of Mr. Universe, at the age of twenty. News of the rising champion traveled fast. Just one year later, the next part of his dream came true. . . .

Arnold was invited to continue his training in America!

He arrived in California in 1968 with all his belongings in two plastic sacks and a gym bag. He didn't have much money, and he didn't speak much English. But Arnold was determined to reach his goals.

He loved doing workouts on famous Muscle Beach while soaking up the sunshine. His nickname was the Austrian Oak because he looked like a big, sturdy tree.

Soon he was hired to star in a movie called *Hercules in New York.* Since Arnold spoke with a thick Austrian accent, the filmmakers used another actor's voice for all his lines. They even changed Arnold's name. They said Schwarzenegger was too strange and wouldn't fit on the movie poster! They called him Arnold Strong instead. When the movie came out in 1970, it was a terrible flop. Did Arnold give up on his dream? No way!

Arnold kept competing and won many titles. At the age of twenty-three, he was the youngest person to ever win Mr. Olympia. When it came to bodybuilding, Arnold was on top. But when it came to acting, he still felt like a beginner.

So Arnold worked hard to improve. He took classes in English, speech, and acting. Eventually, he was hired to play the lead role in a movie called *Conan the Barbarian*. His character was a muscular hero. It was the perfect role for Arnold. And this time, the movie was a big success!

Arnold had always dreamed of being a movie star—and now he was one!

In 1983, Arnold became a US citizen. That day, he couldn't stop smiling! He celebrated with his girlfriend, Maria Shriver, a news reporter and the niece of President John F. Kennedy. The couple later married and had four children.

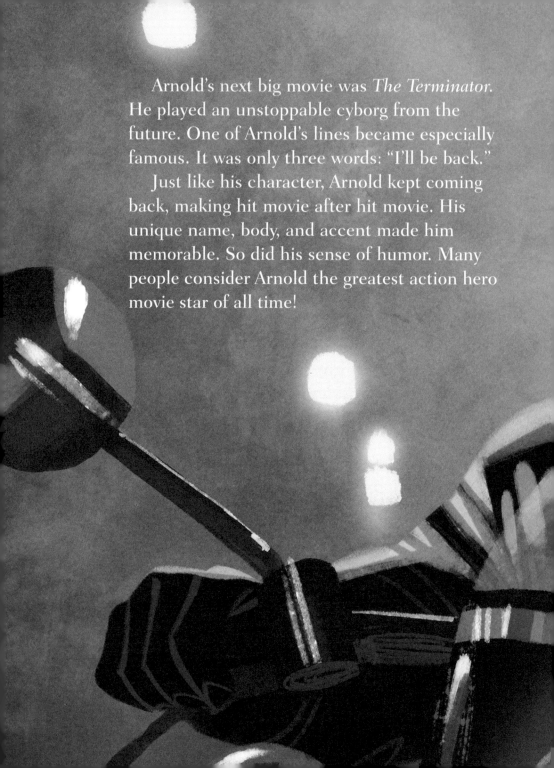

Arnold's next big movie was *The Terminator*. He played an unstoppable cyborg from the future. One of Arnold's lines became especially famous. It was only three words: "I'll be back."

Just like his character, Arnold kept coming back, making hit movie after hit movie. His unique name, body, and accent made him memorable. So did his sense of humor. Many people consider Arnold the greatest action hero movie star of all time!

Meanwhile, he inspired others to stay fit and active. In 1990, President George H. W. Bush appointed him the chairman of the President's Council on Physical Fitness and Sports. Arnold led workouts on the White House lawn. He also supported the Special Olympics and the Inner-City Games to give all kids a chance to exercise and build confidence.

Arnold grew more interested in politics. He admired former President Ronald Reagan, who had also been an actor. In 2003, Arnold ran for governor of California—and won. People nicknamed him "The Governator." He served for eight years and signed laws to help protect the environment and make school meals more nutritious.

Arnold is an example of the ultimate immigrant success story. The father of five has been a world-famous bodybuilder, movie star, business owner, and politician. And it all started because a poor boy from a small village dared to dream big!

Strength DOES NOT COME FROM WINNING. YOUR Struggles DEVELOP YOUR STRENGTHS.